A-Z Vehicle Coloring Book

Copyright @2023 Vanitha Vaidialingam
All rights reserved
No part of this book shall be copied or transmitted in any fashion whatsover without the written permission form the author.

Ambulance

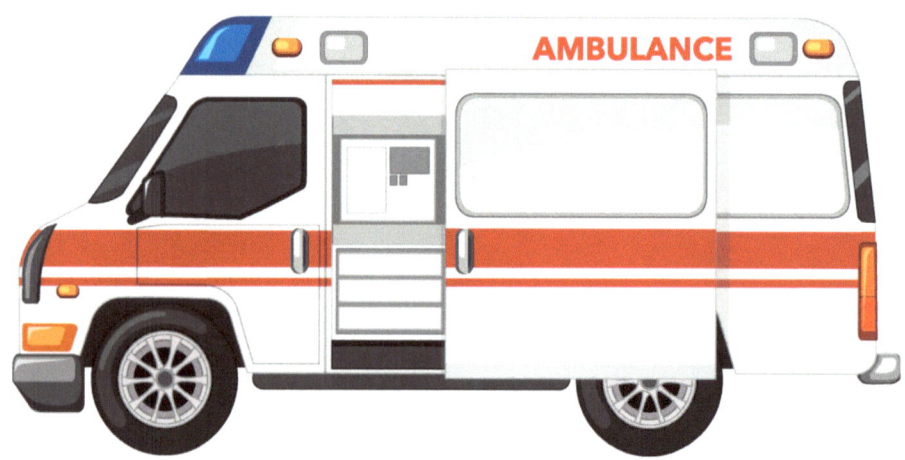

Aa

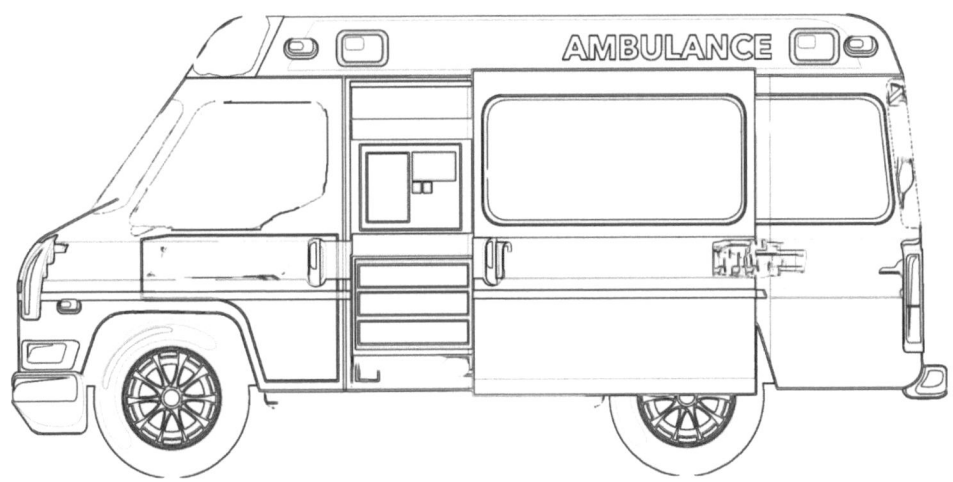

Bulldozer

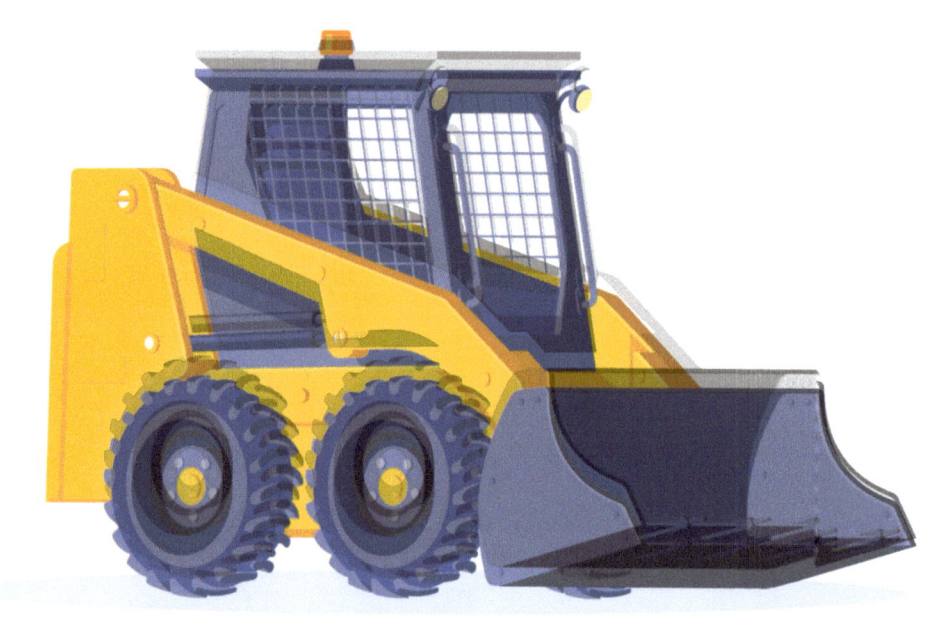

Bb

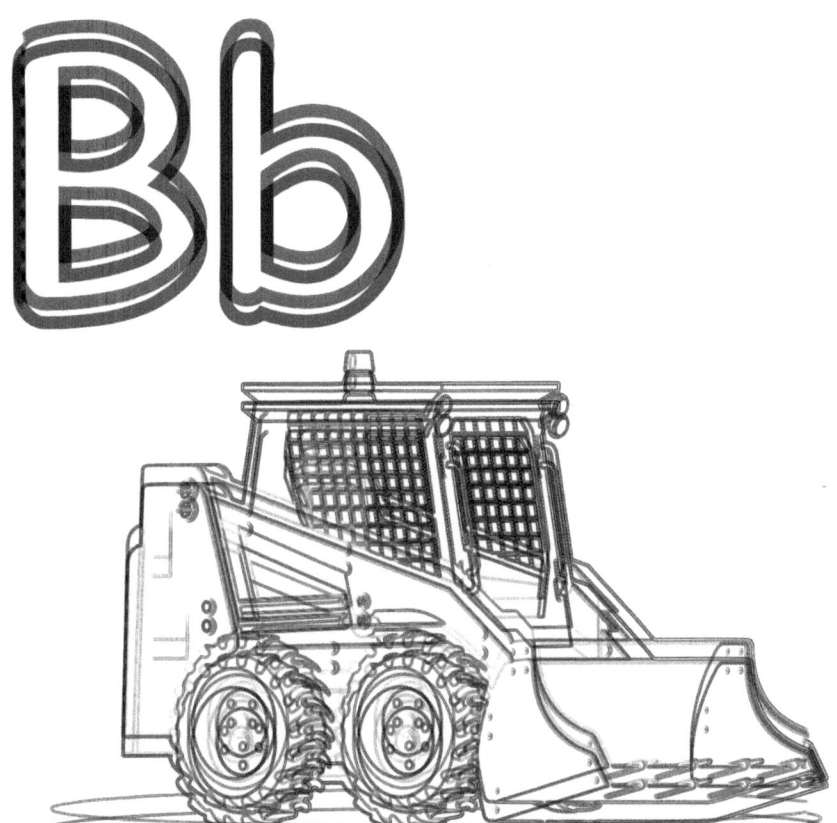

Crane

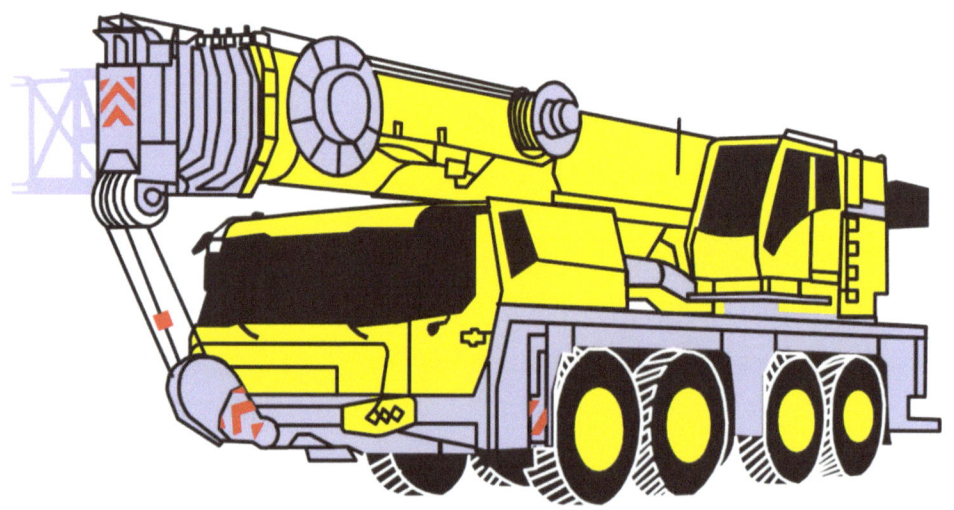

Cc

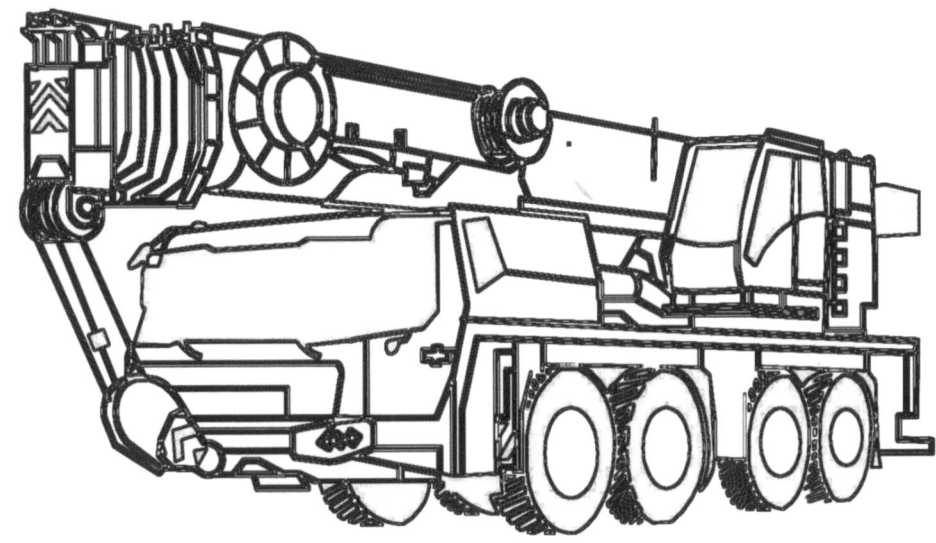

Dump truck

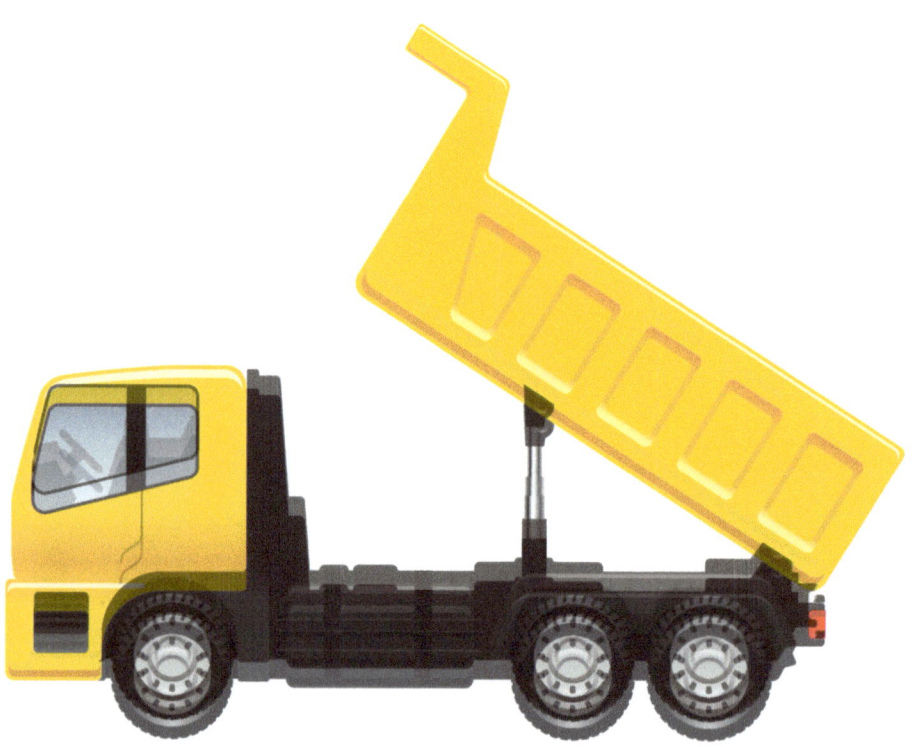

Dd

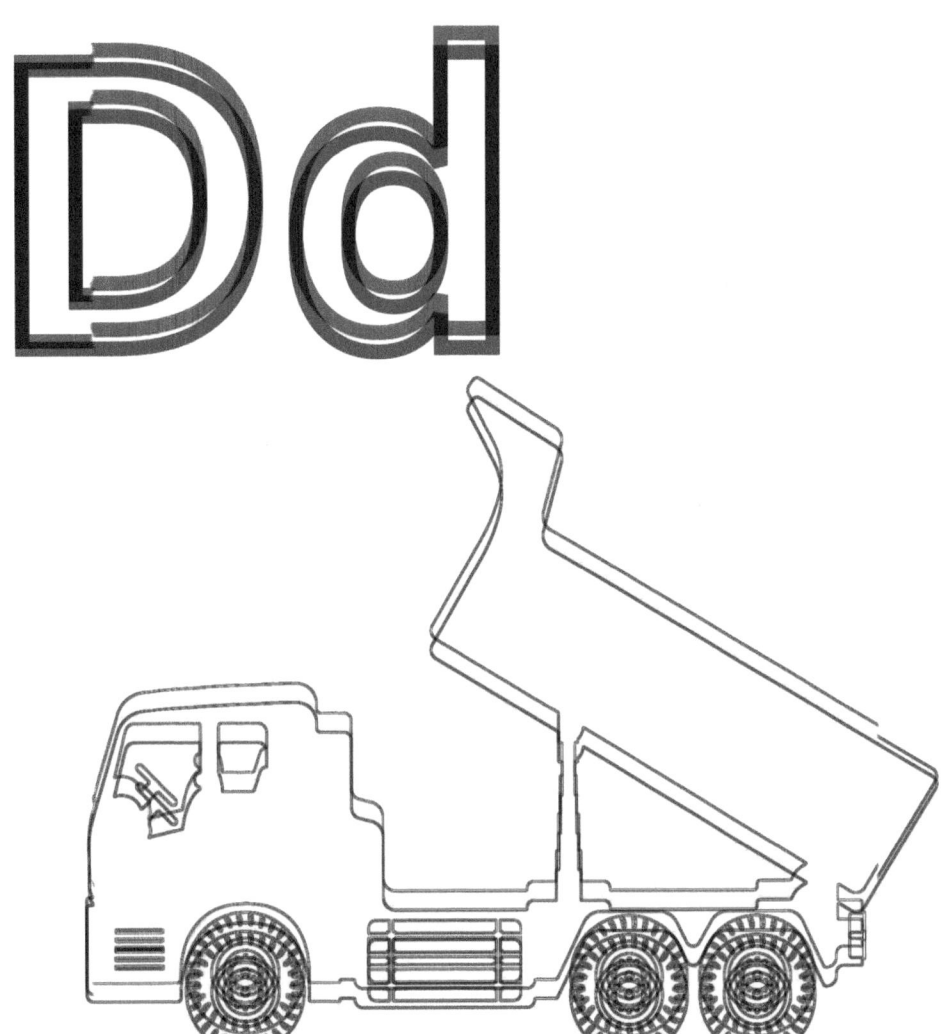

Excavator

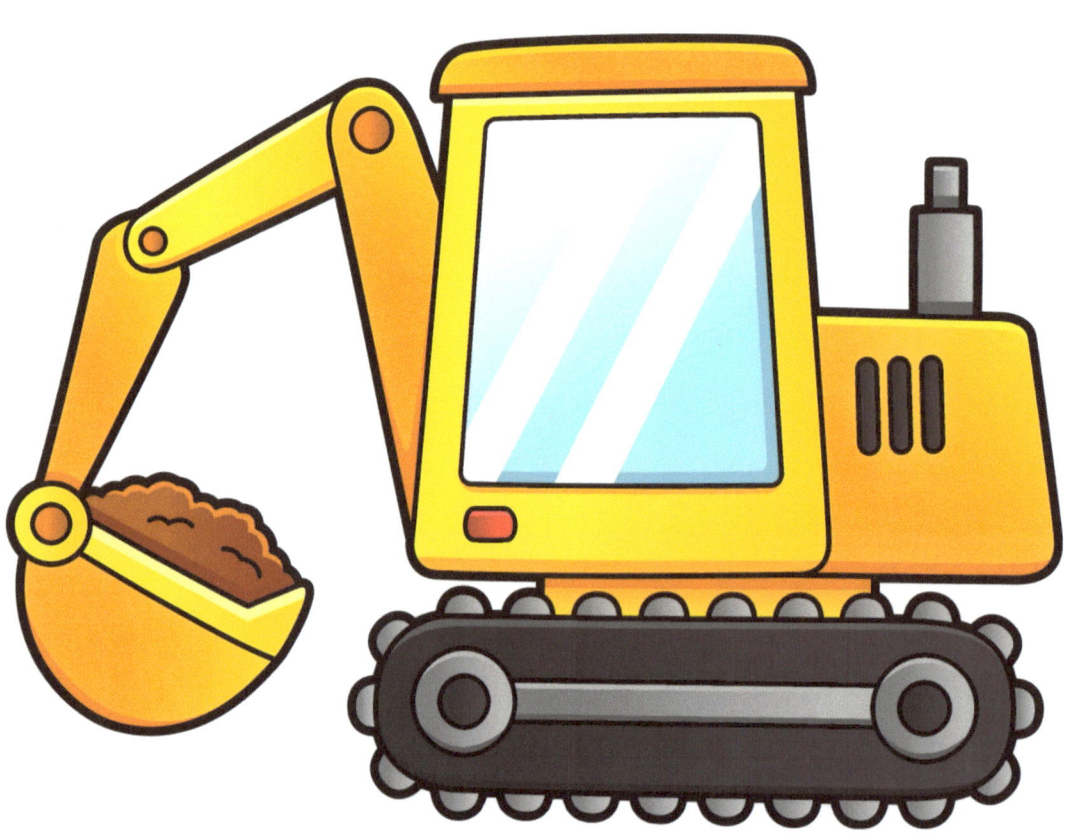

Ee

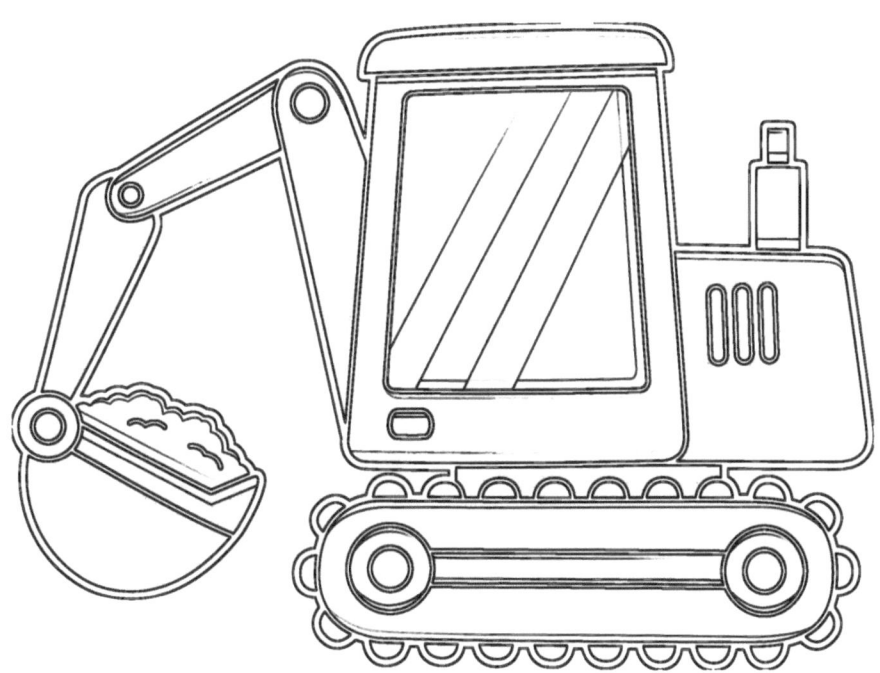

Fire truck

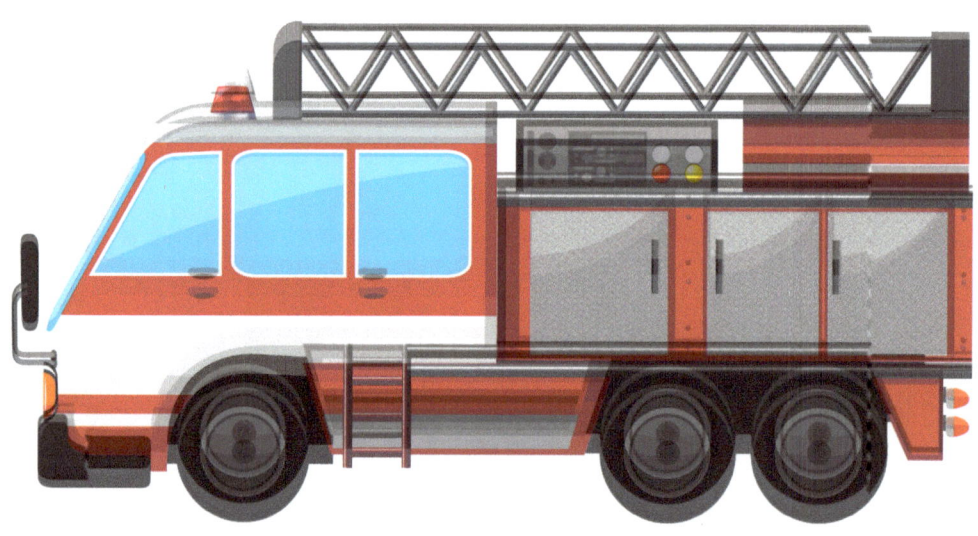

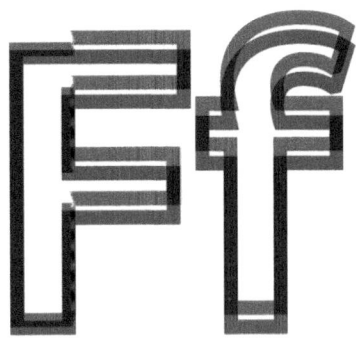

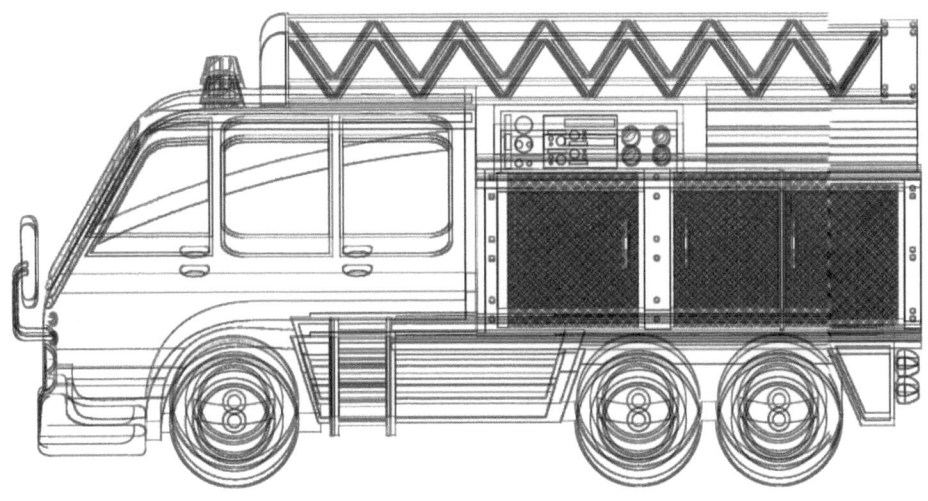

Goods transport truck

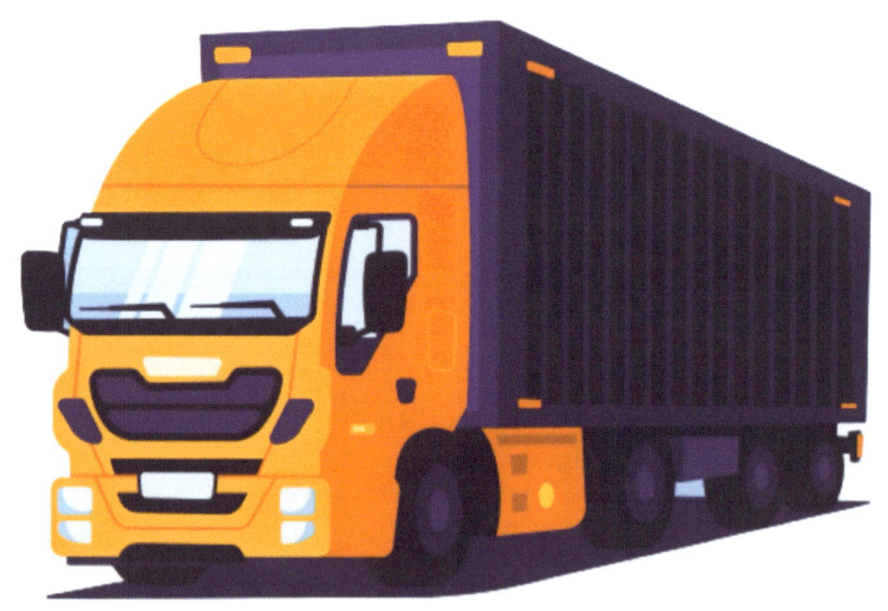

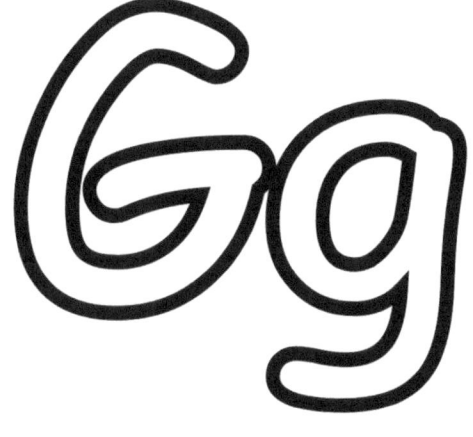
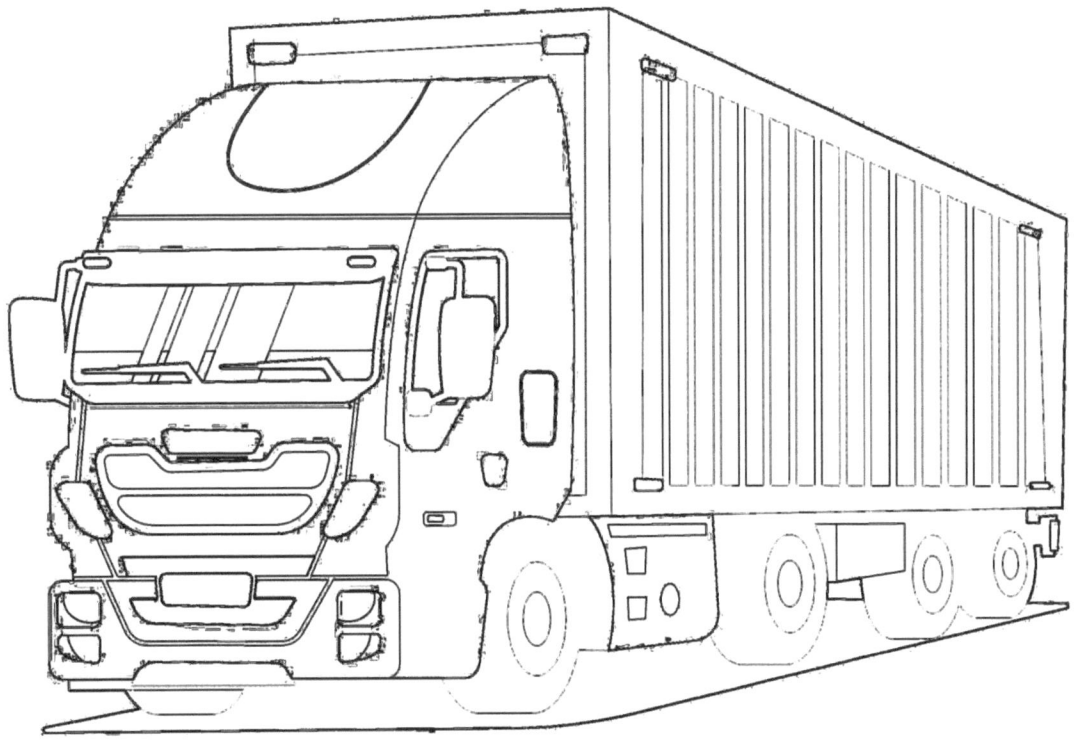

Helicopter

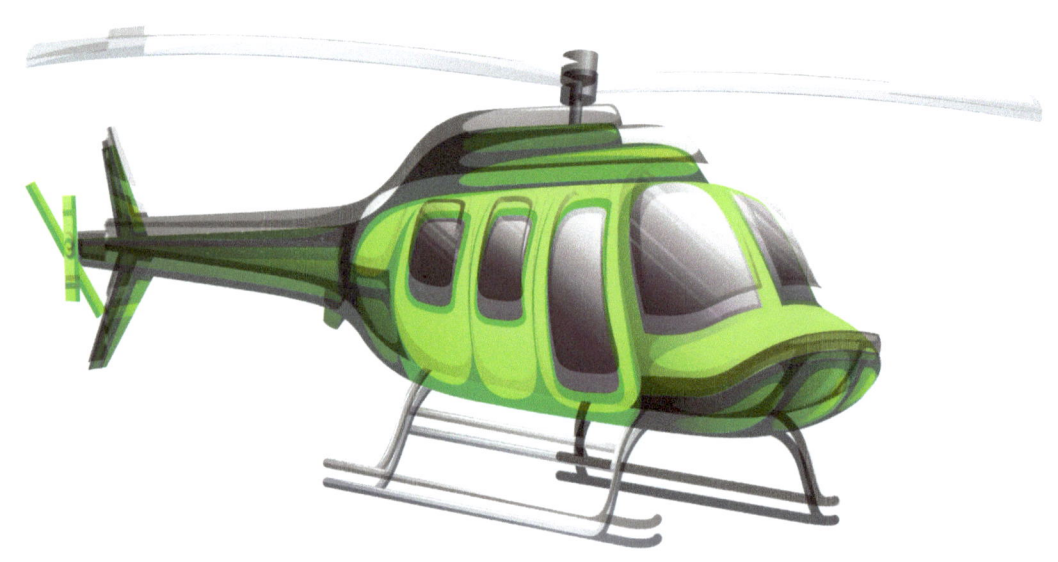

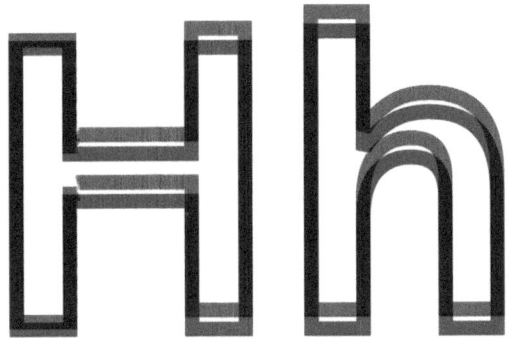

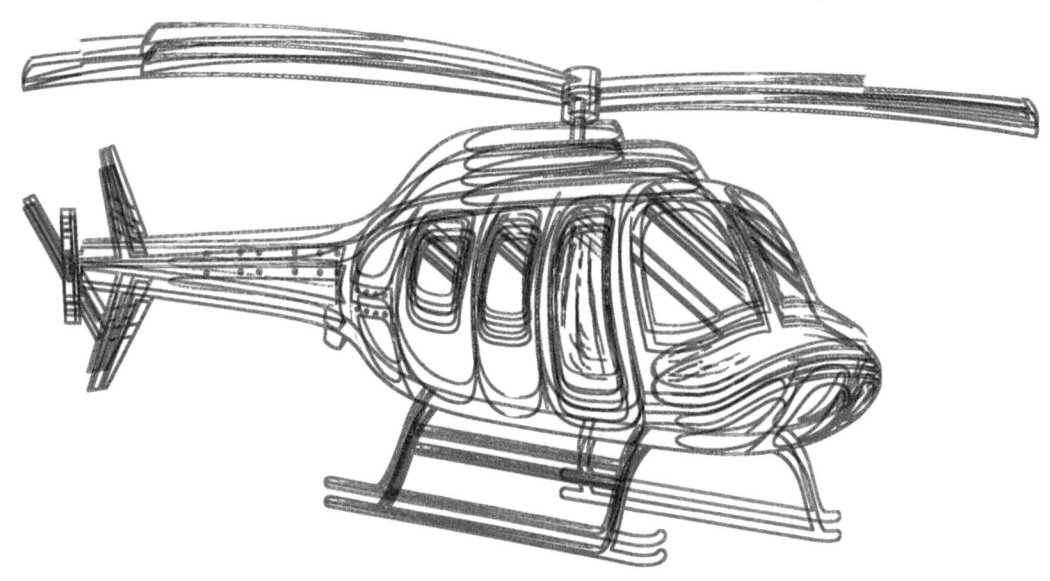

ice-cream truck

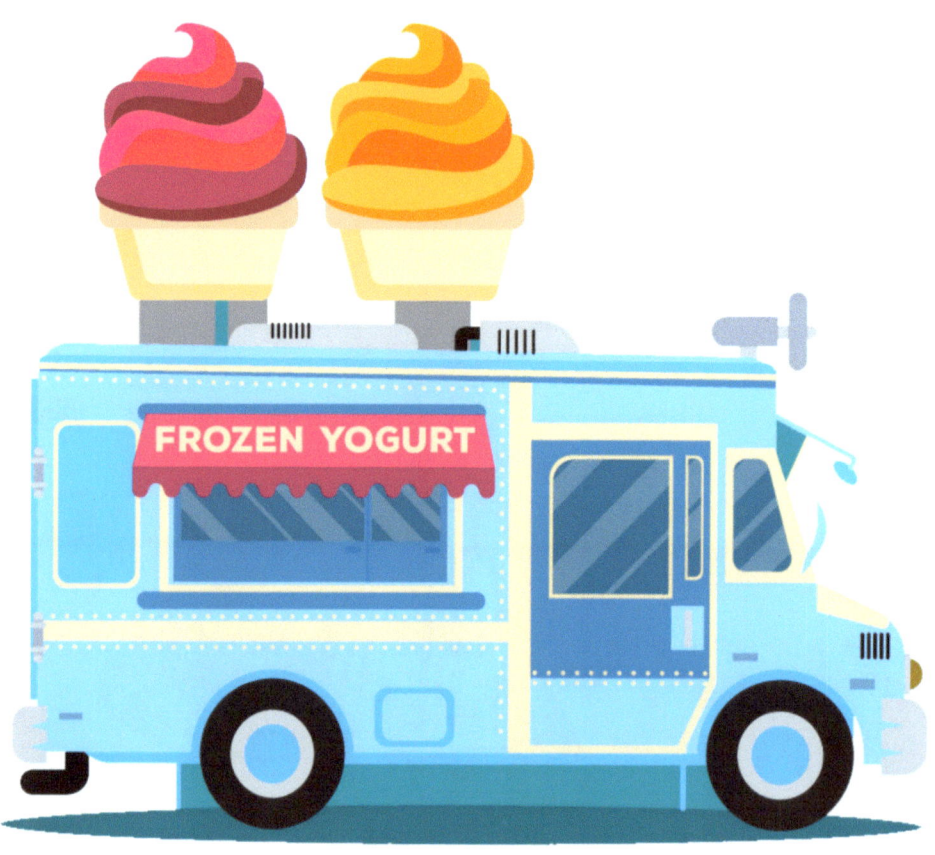

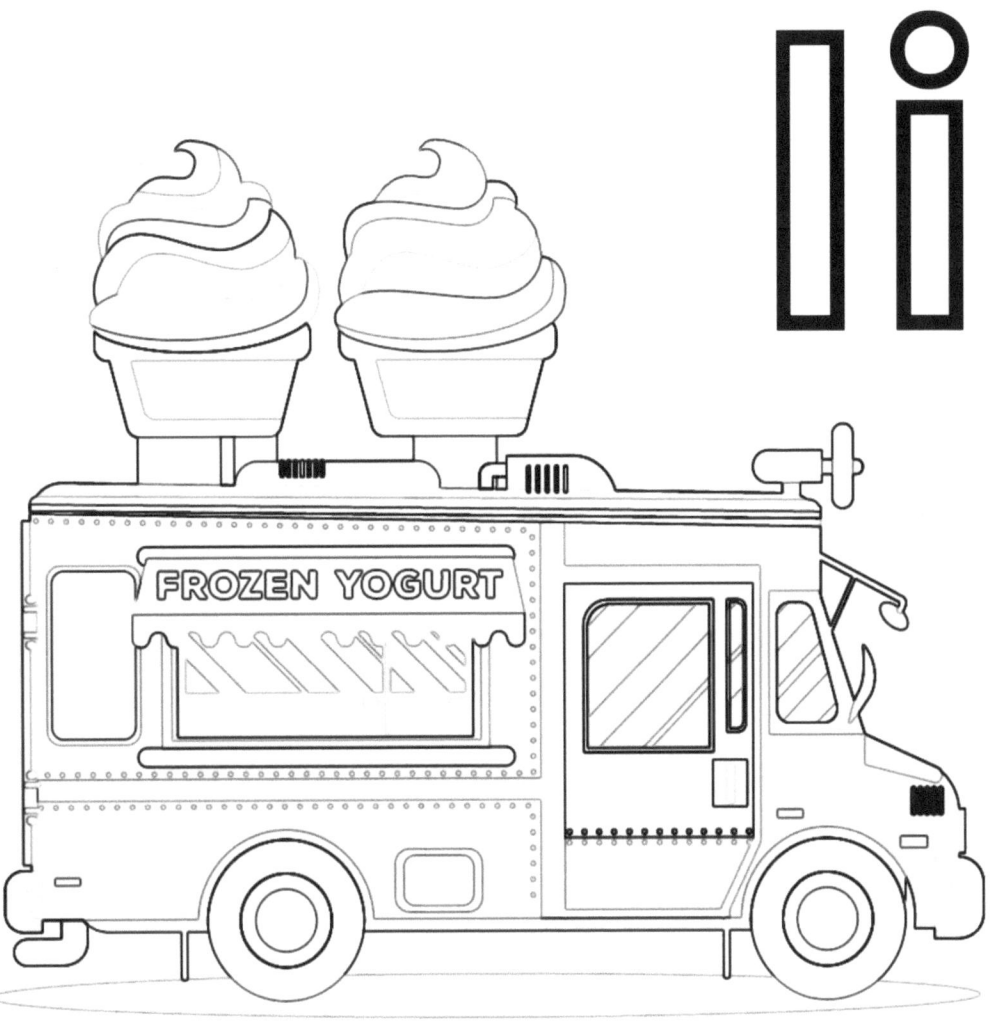

Jeep

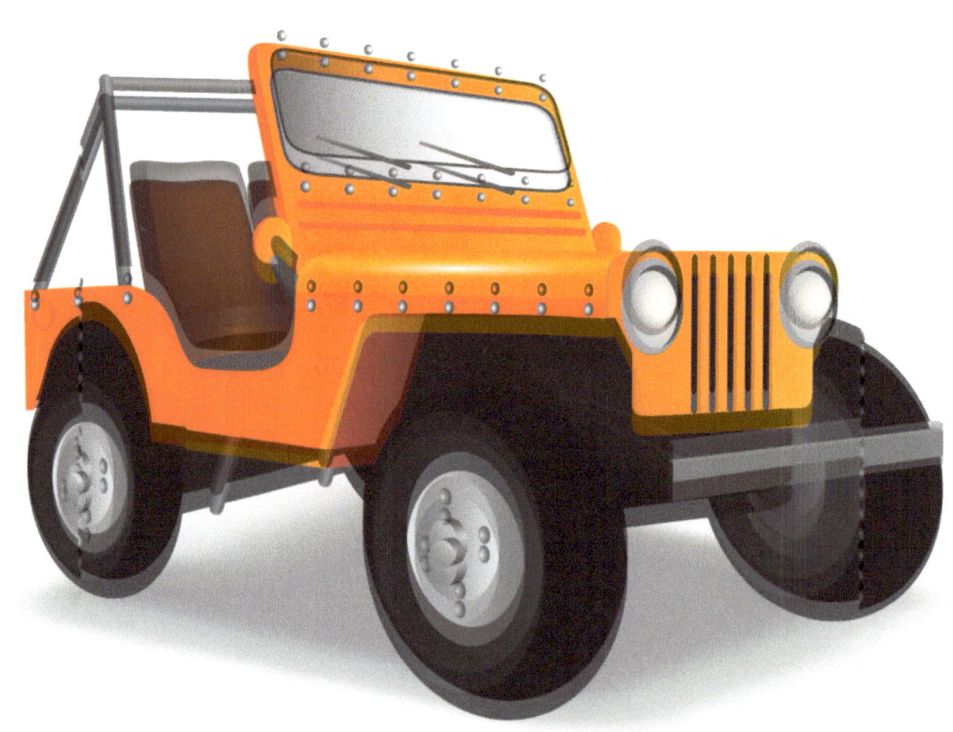

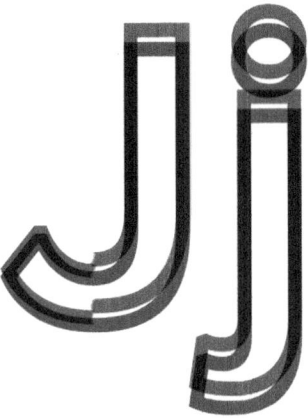

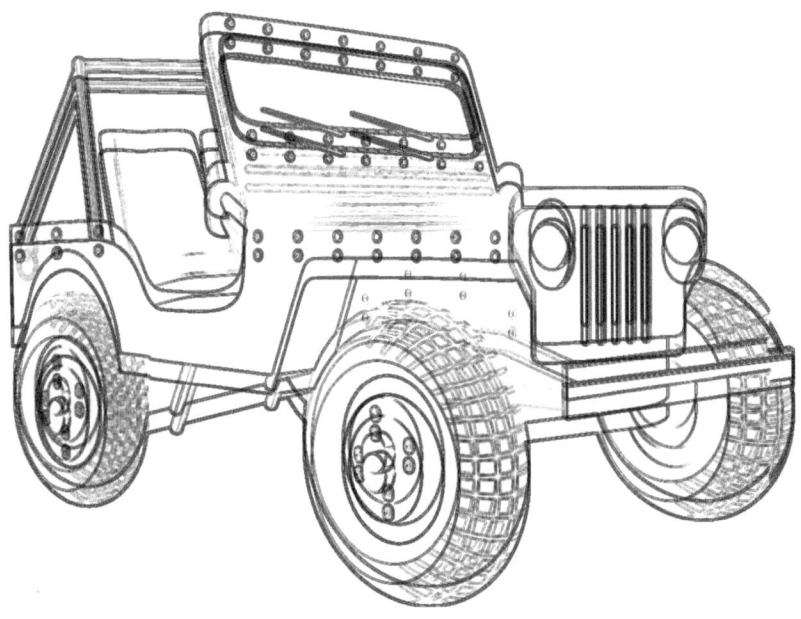

Kayak

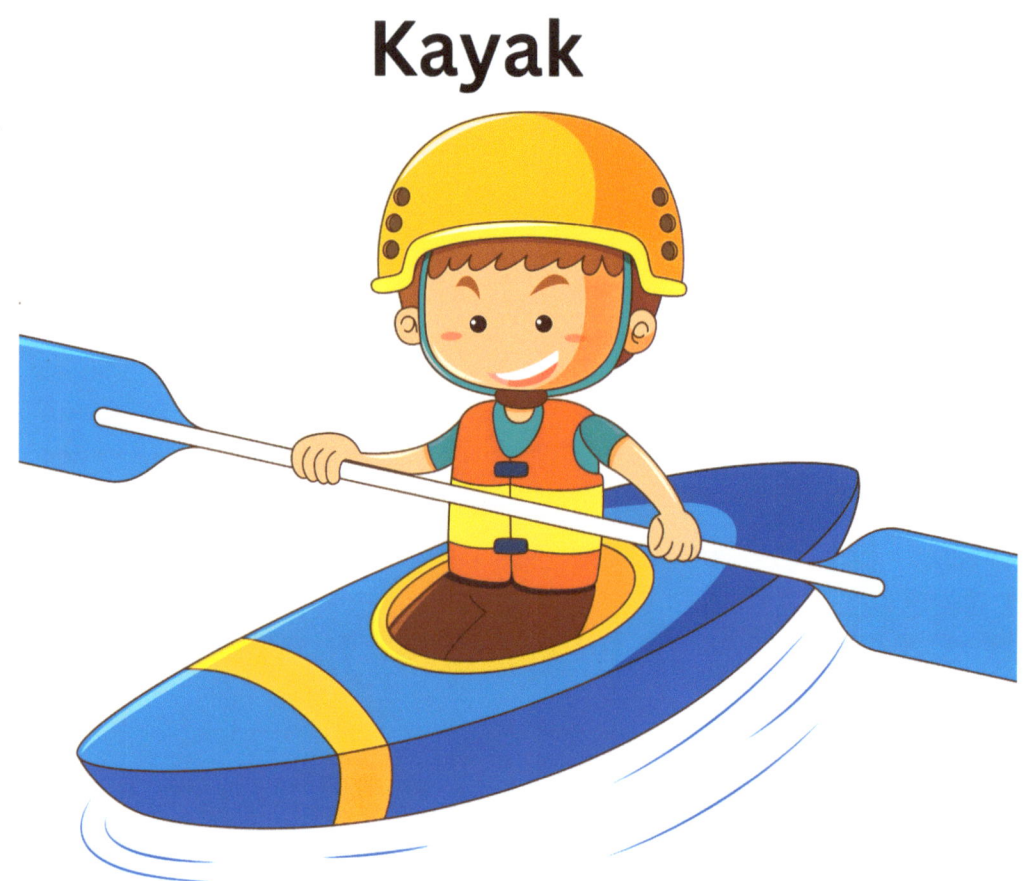

Kk

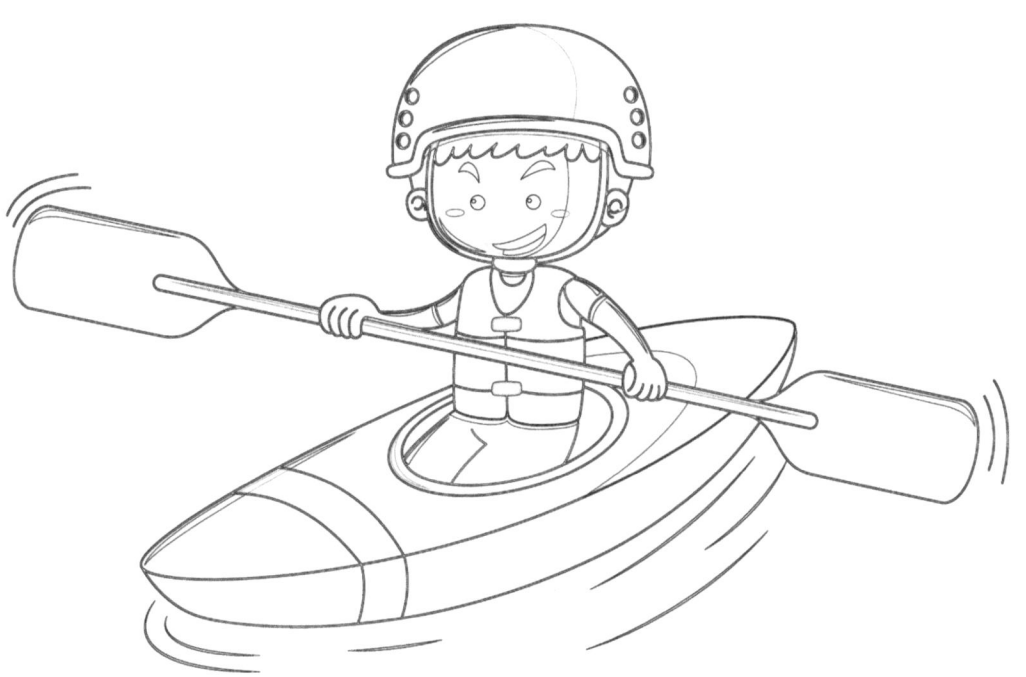

Limousine

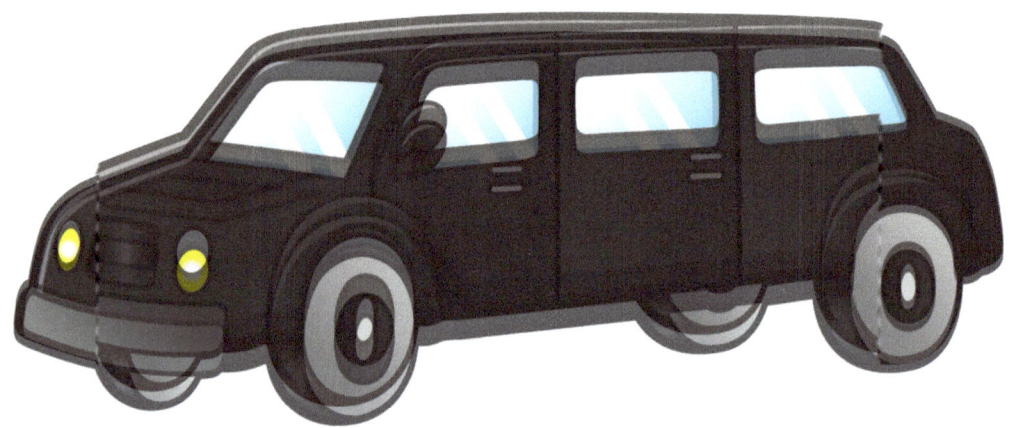

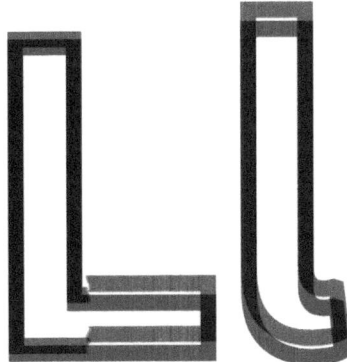

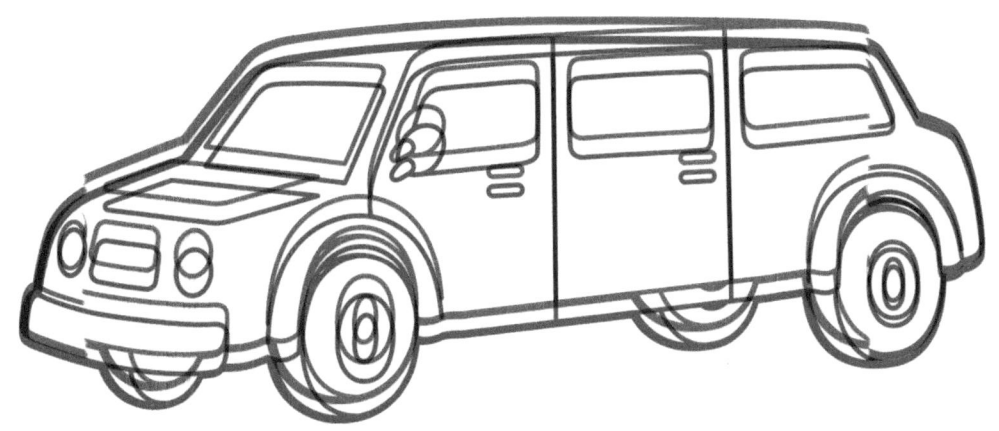

Motor cycle

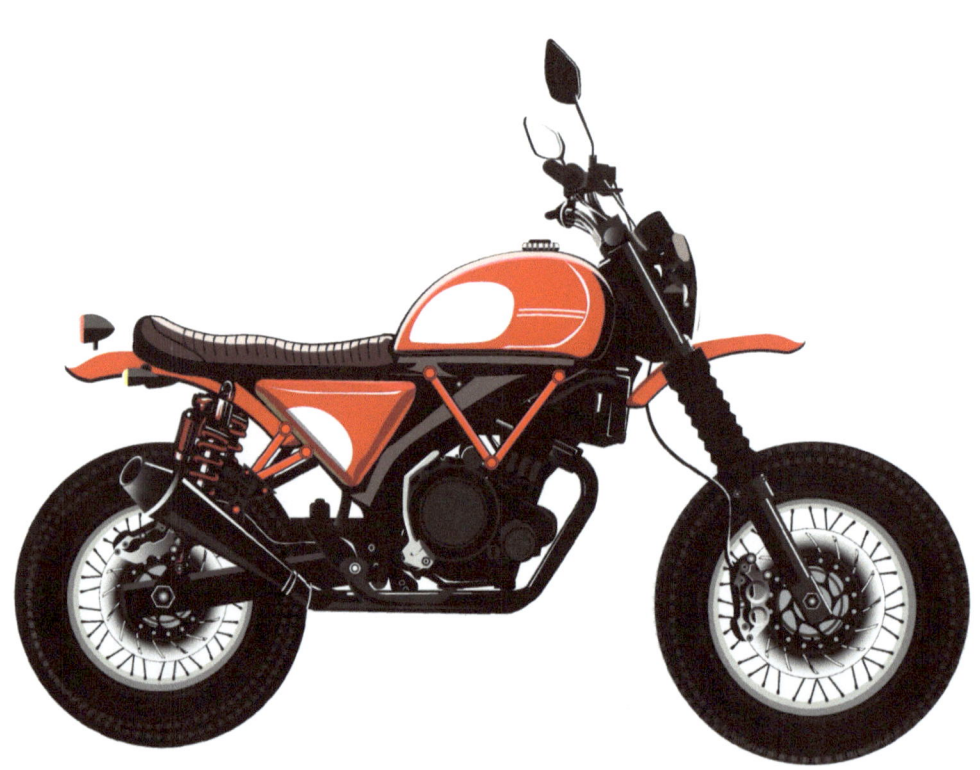

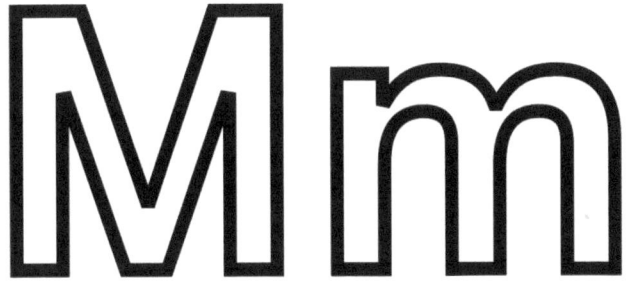
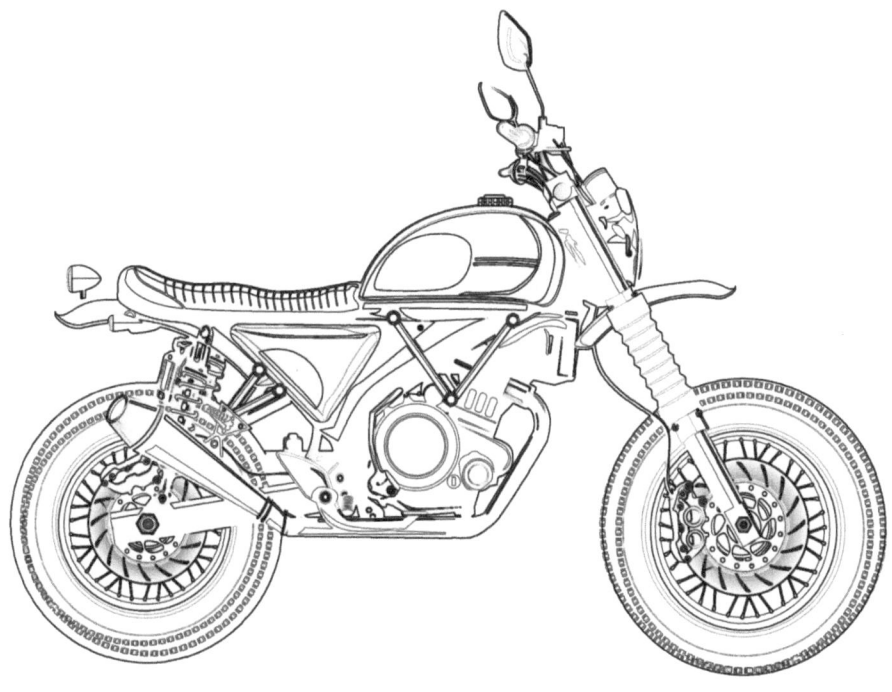

Naval Ship

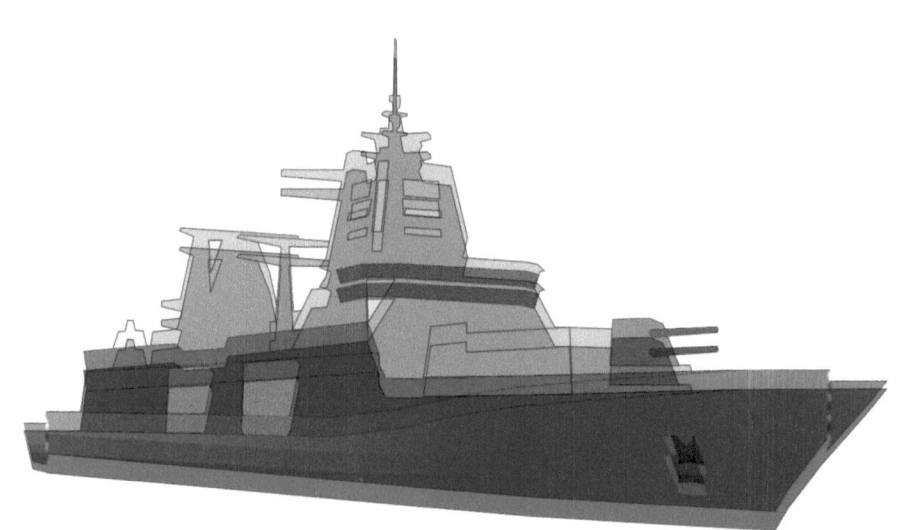

Nn

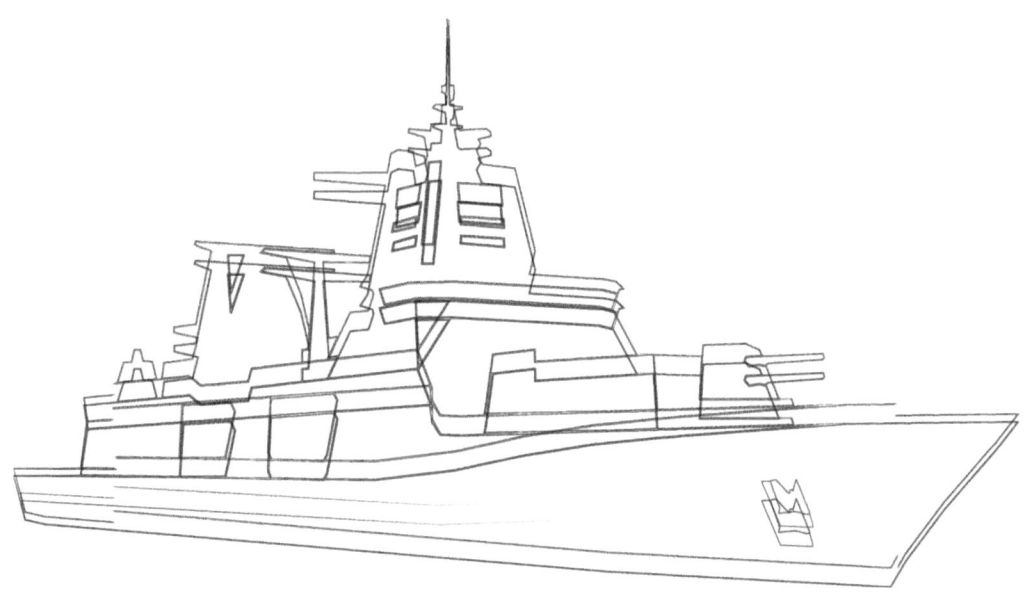

oxcart

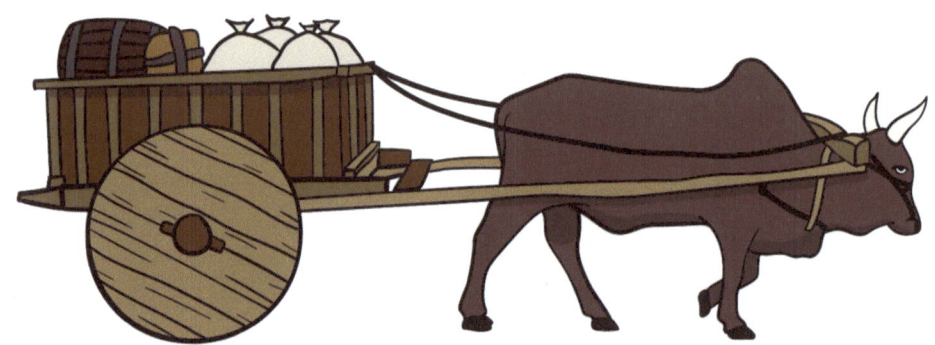

Oo

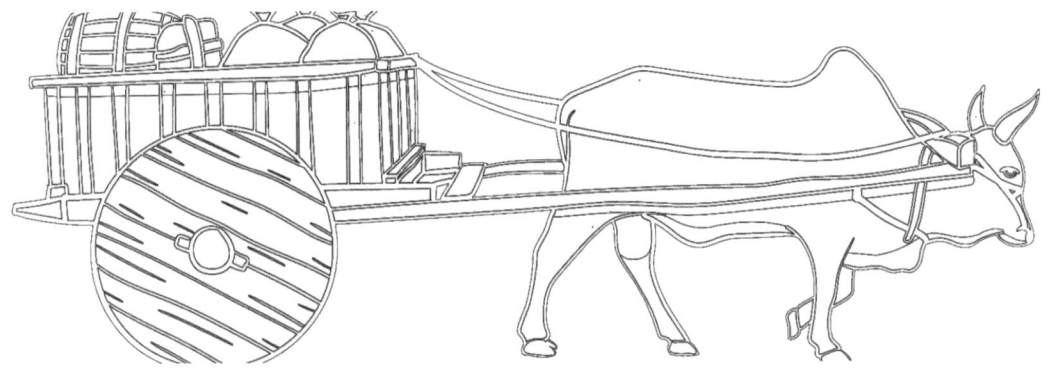

Police Car

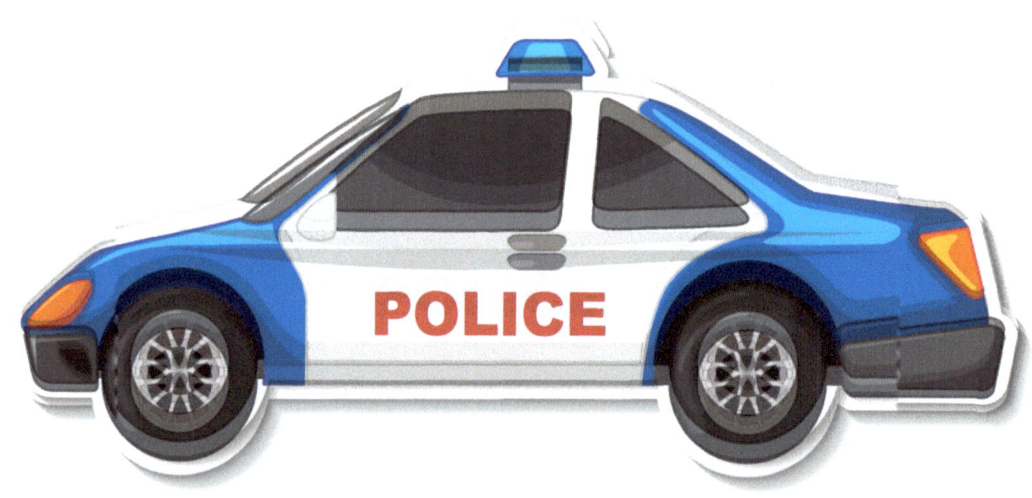

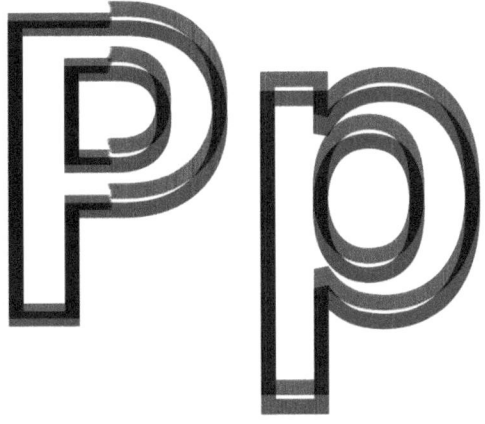
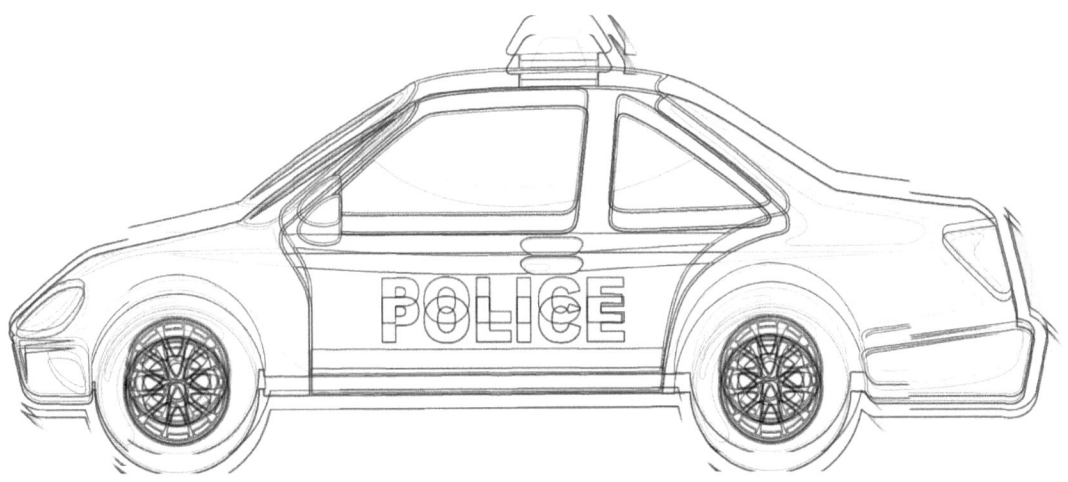

Quad Bike

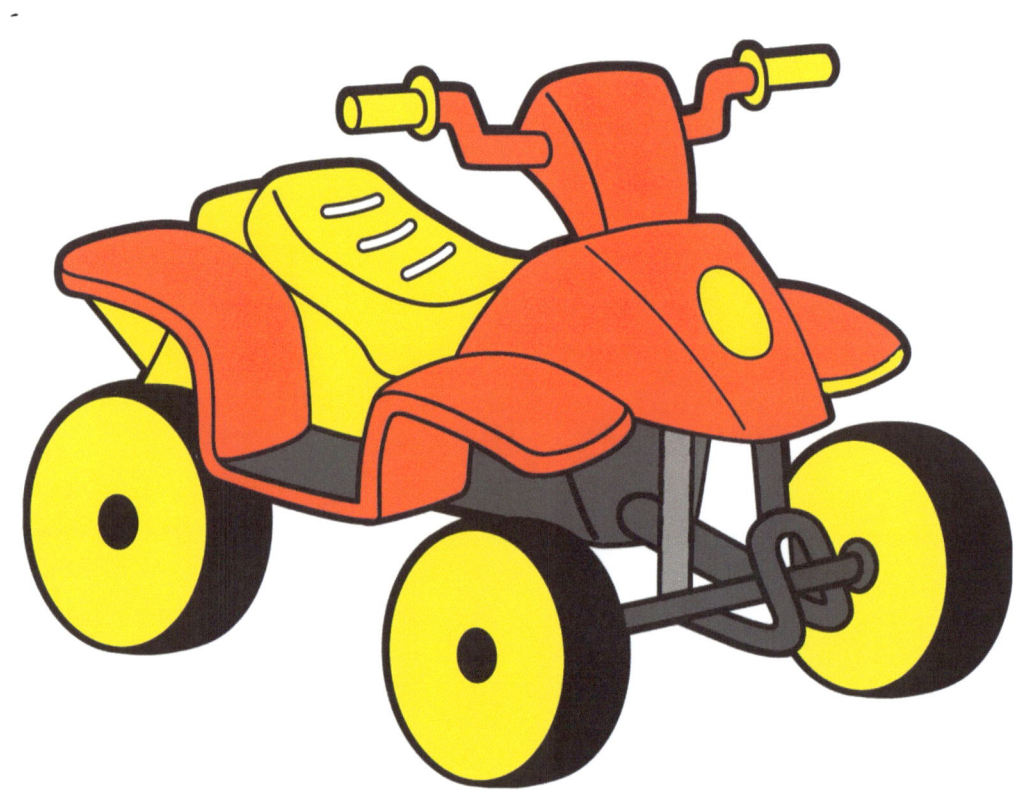

Qq

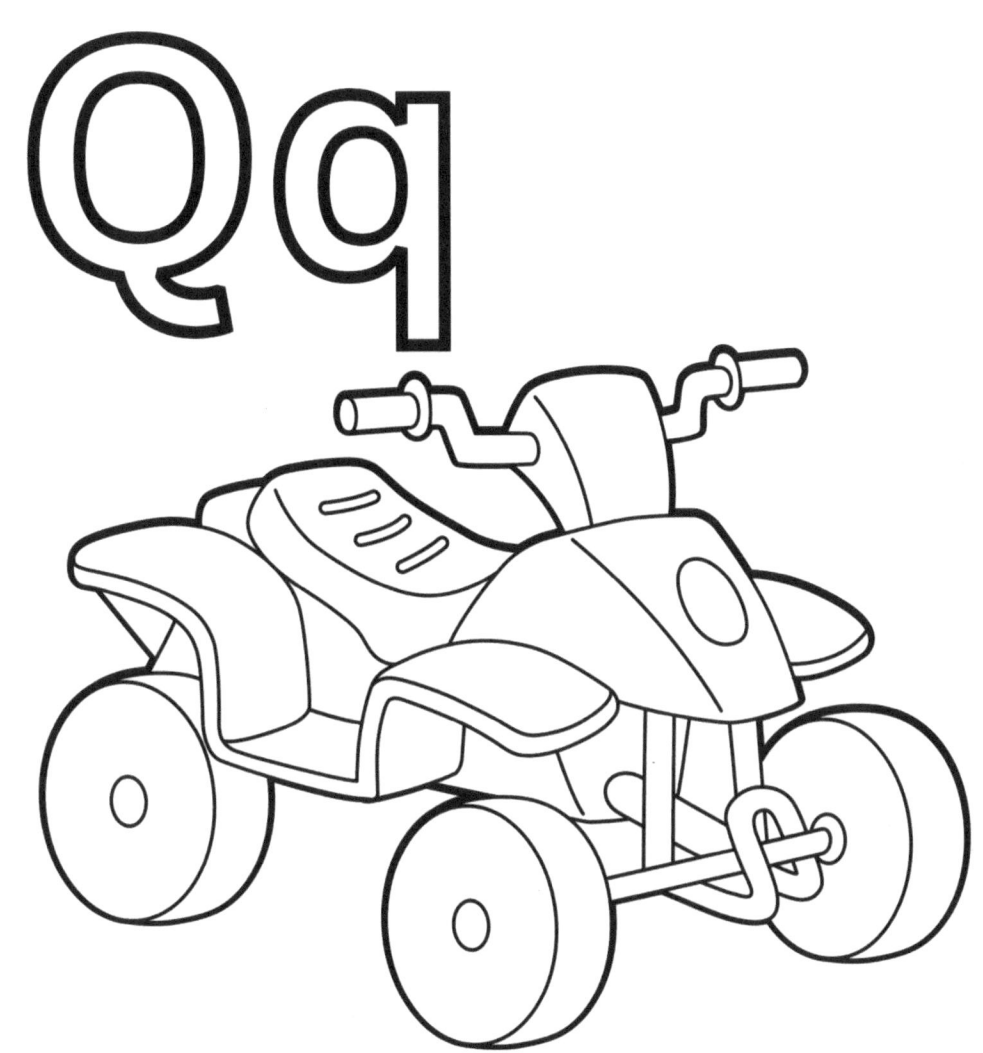

Racing car

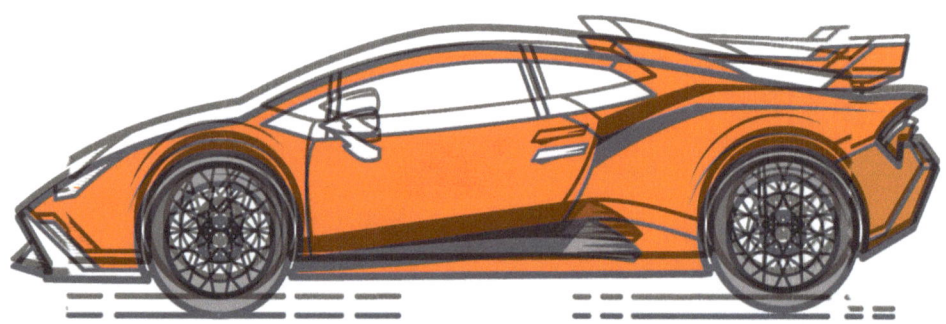

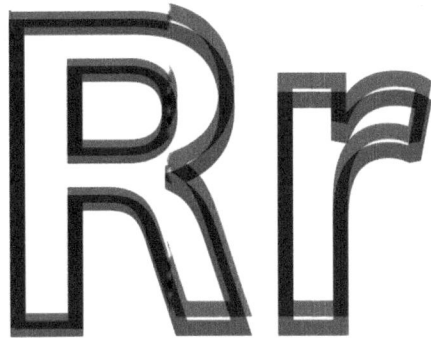

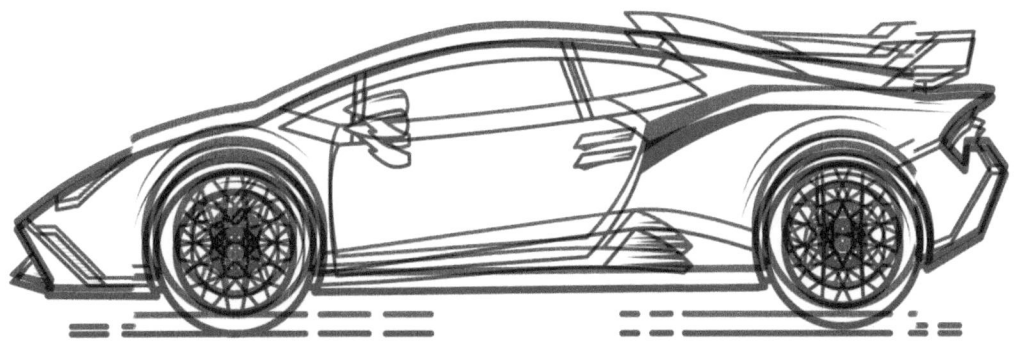

Skate board

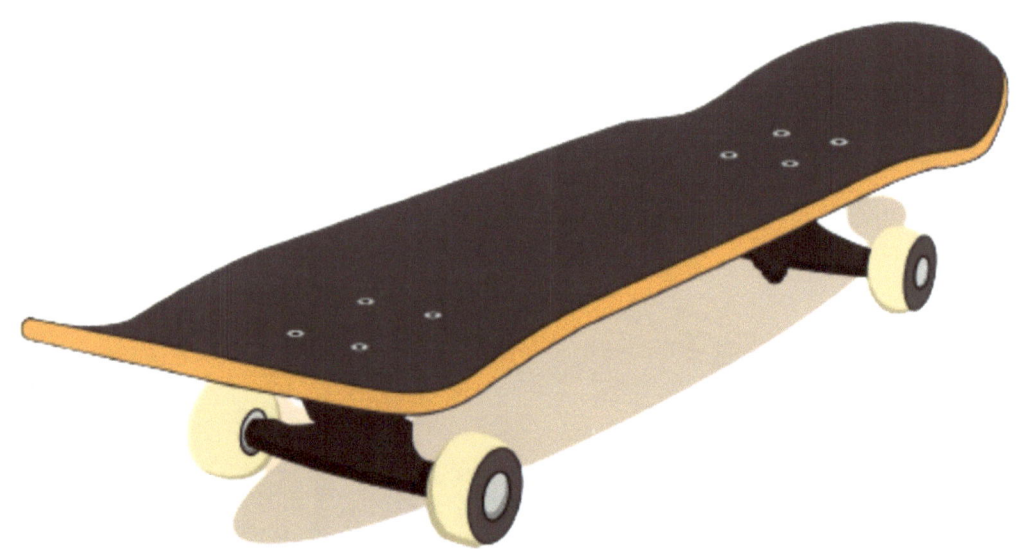

Ss

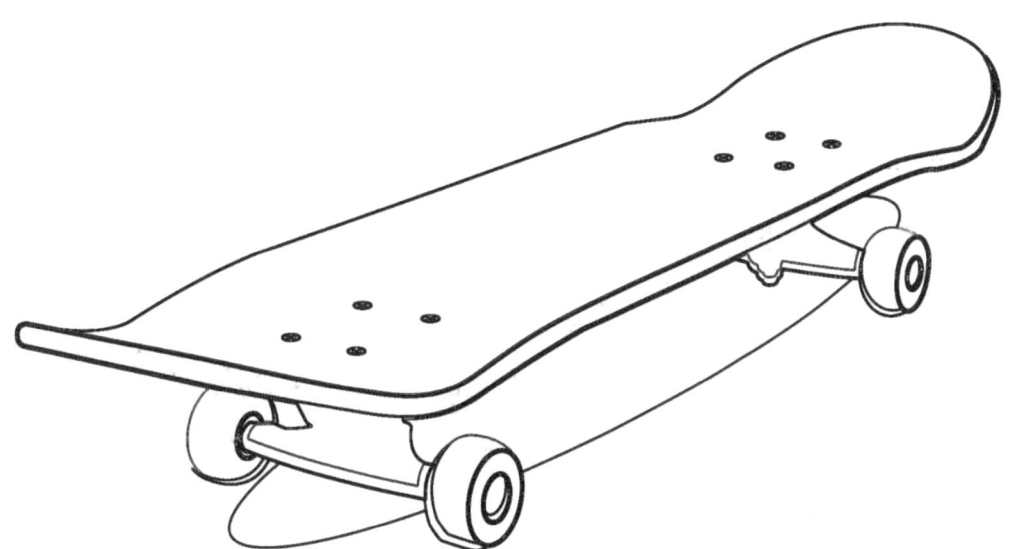

Tractor

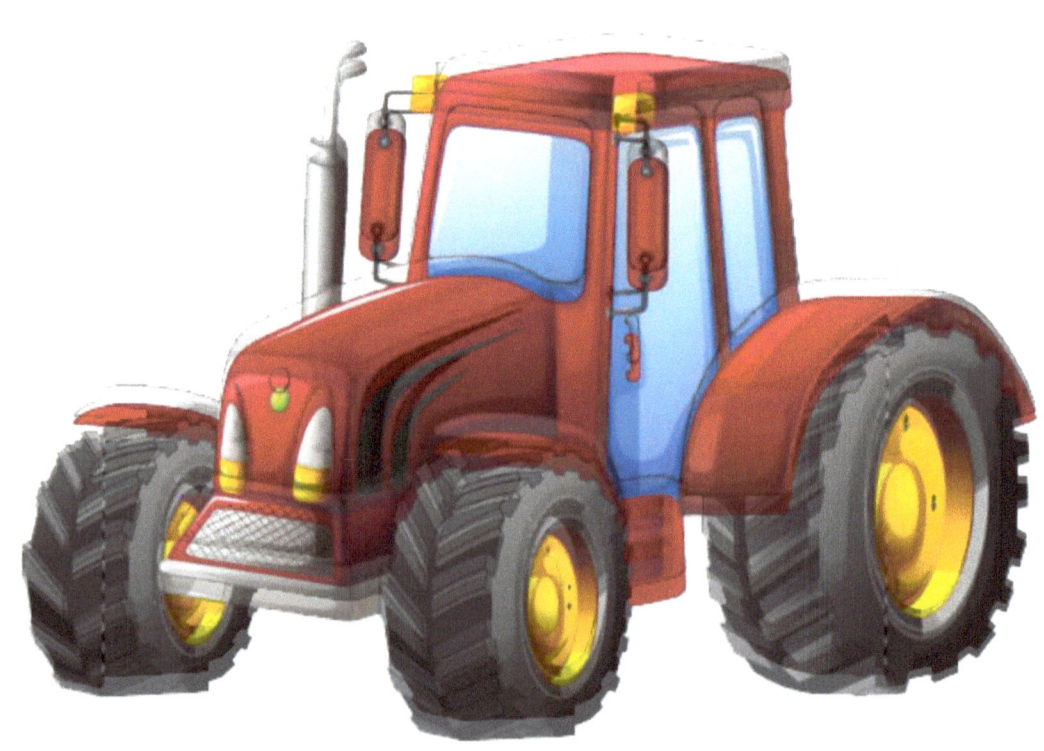

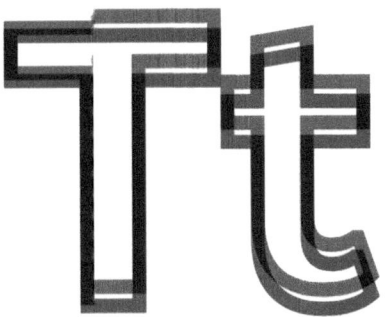

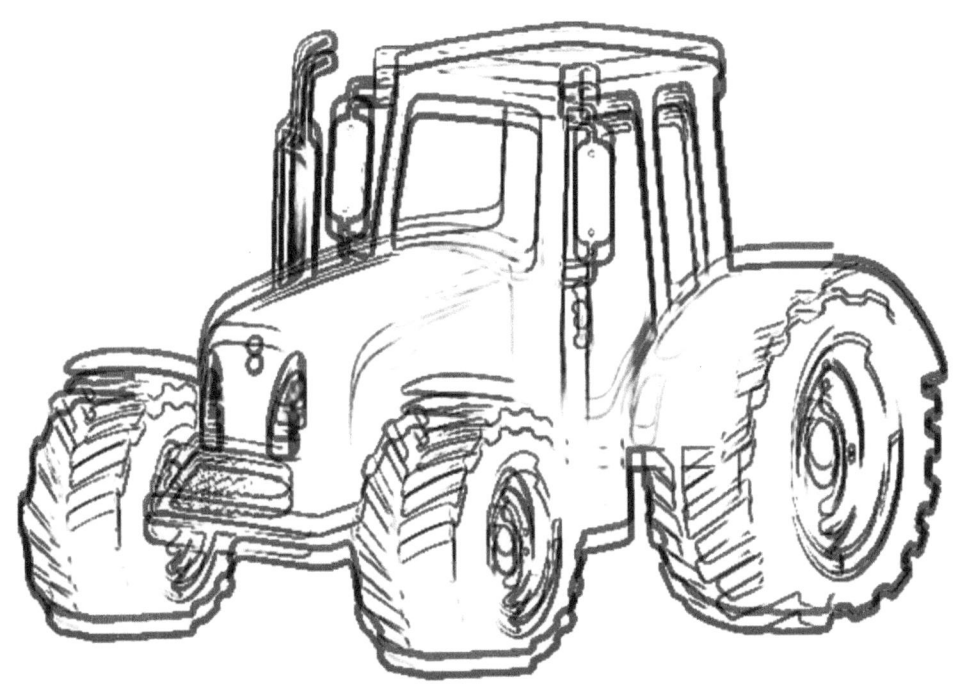

Unicycle

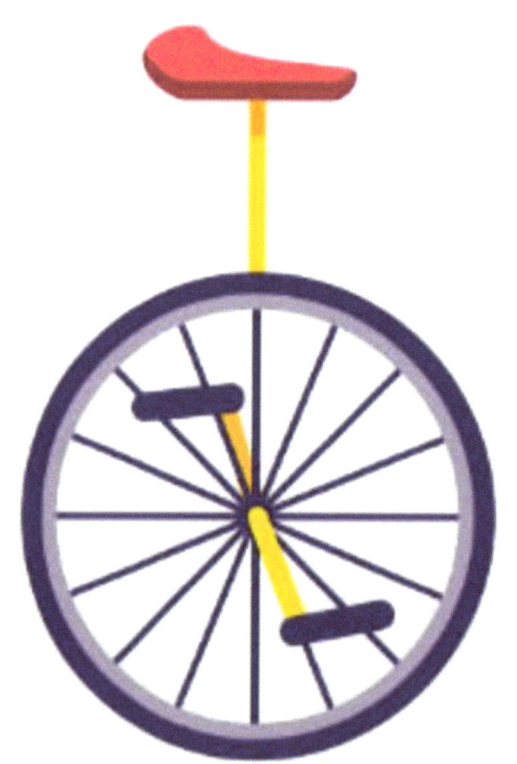

Uu

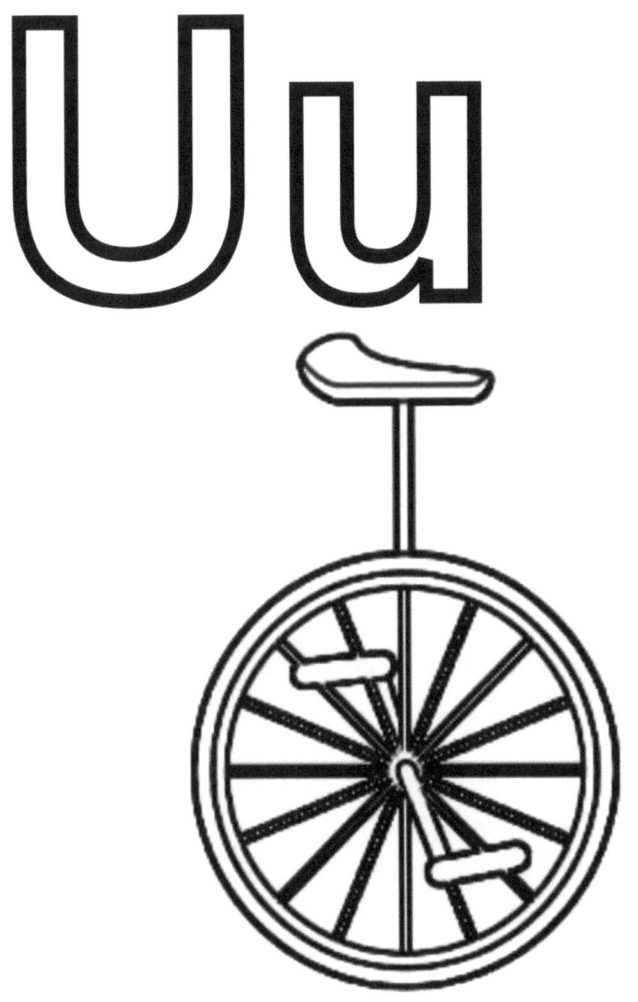

Van

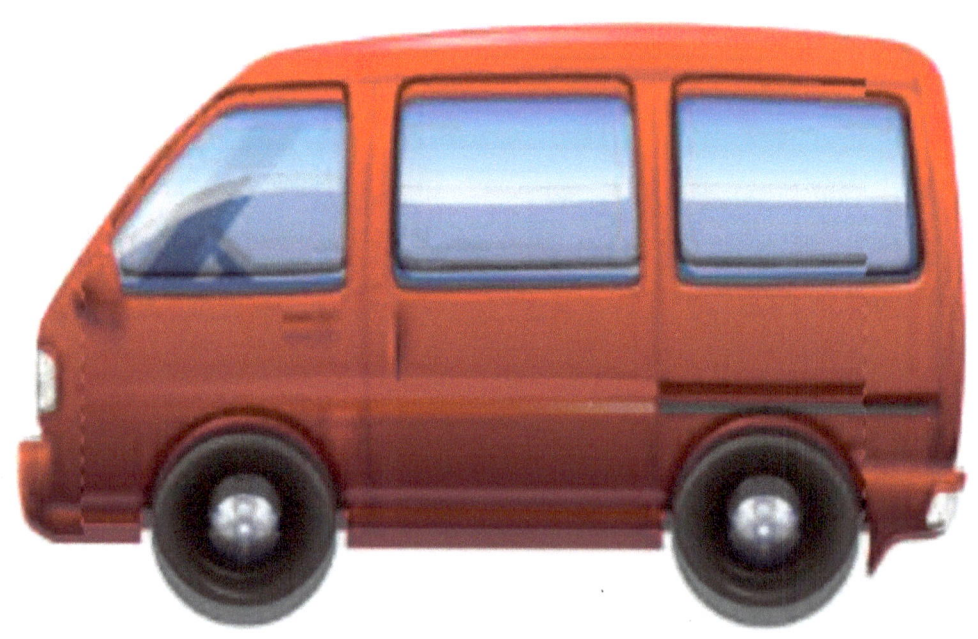

Vv

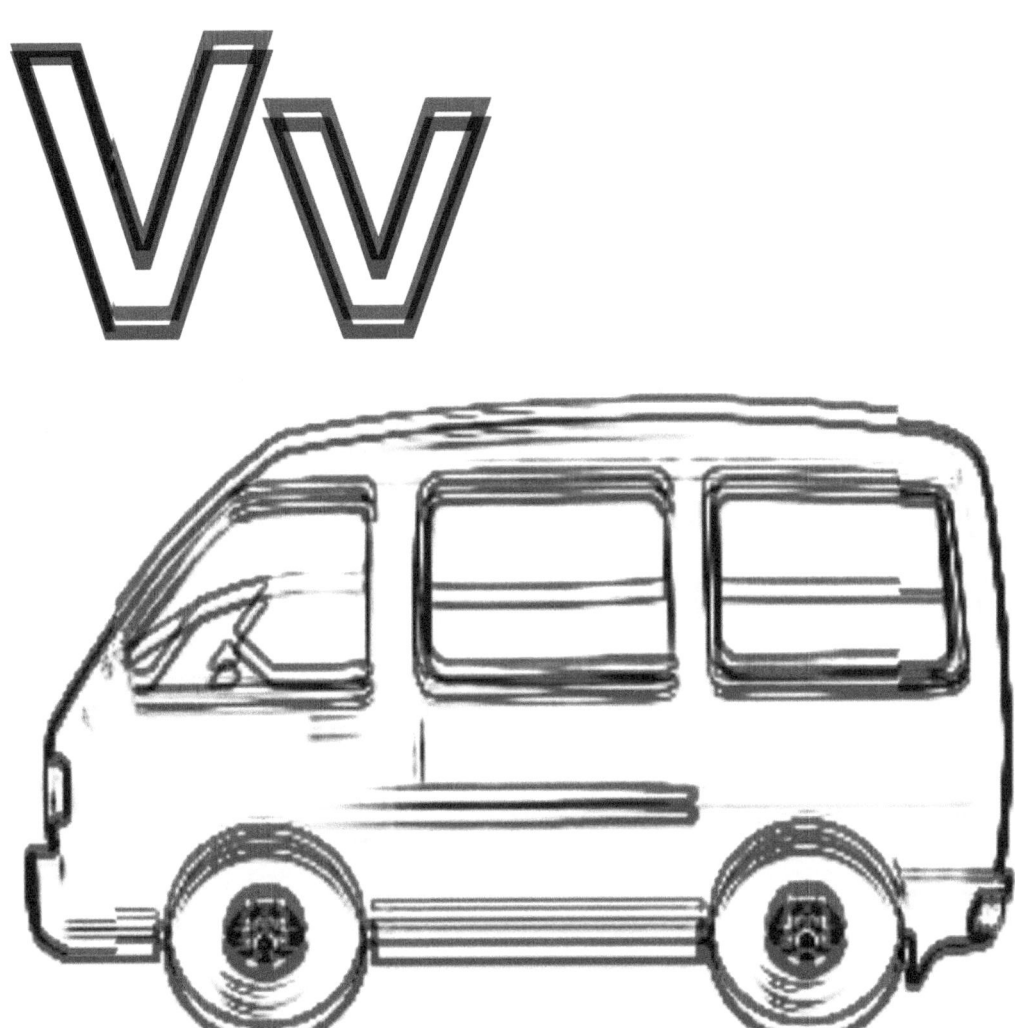

Wagon

Ww

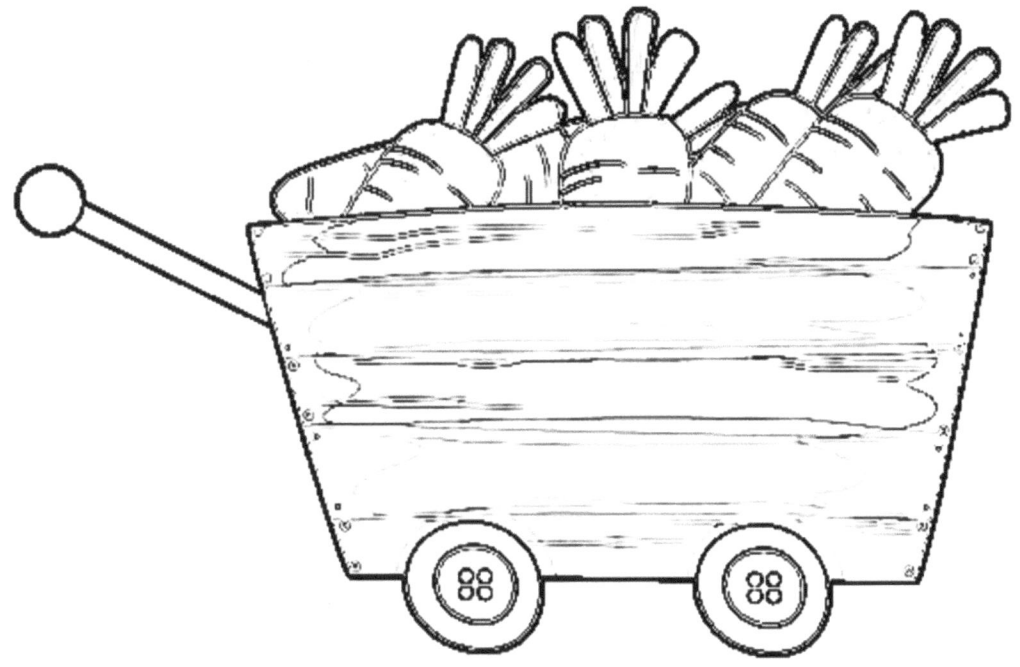

XRAY Truck

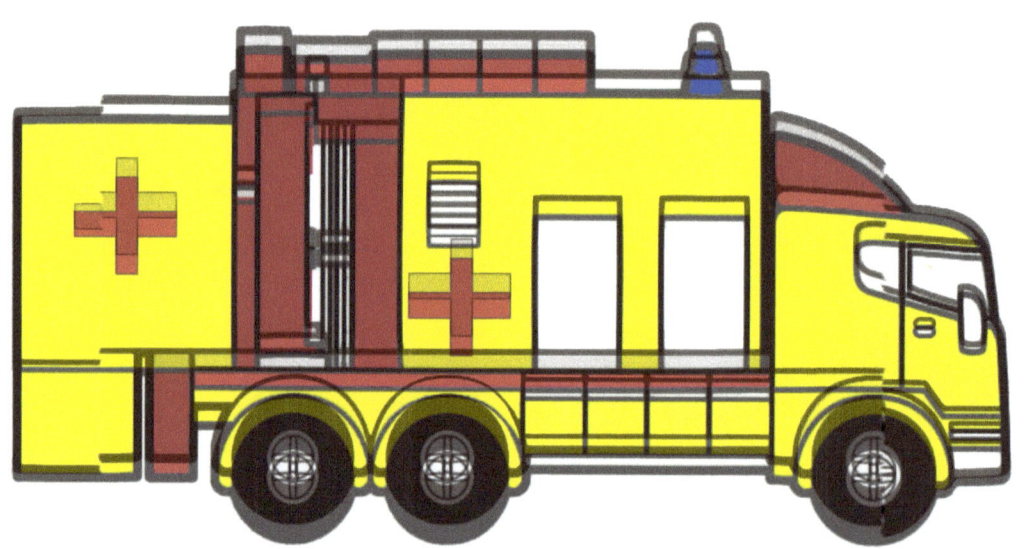

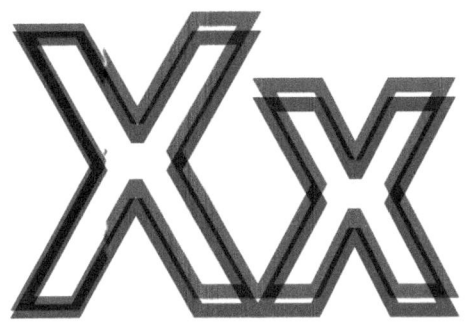

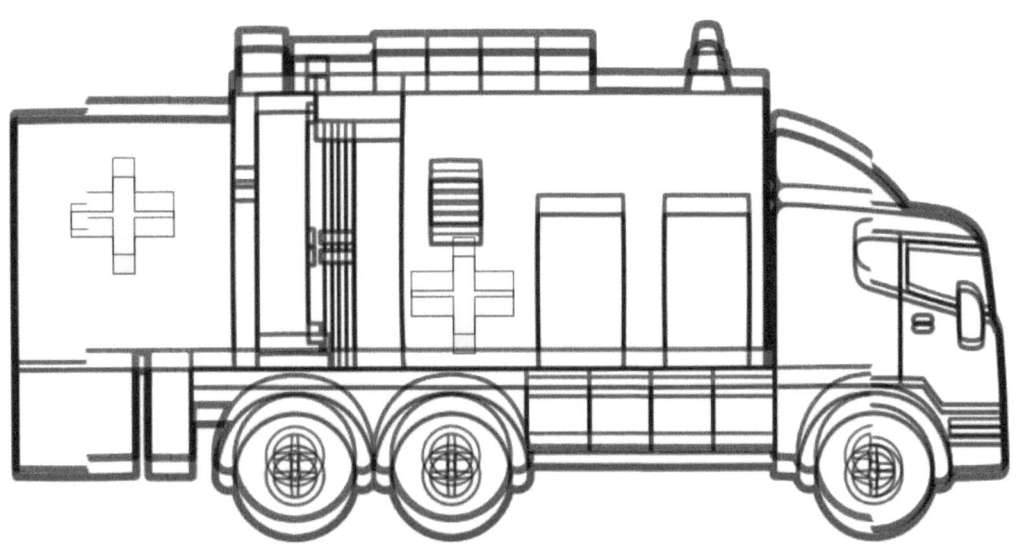

Yatch

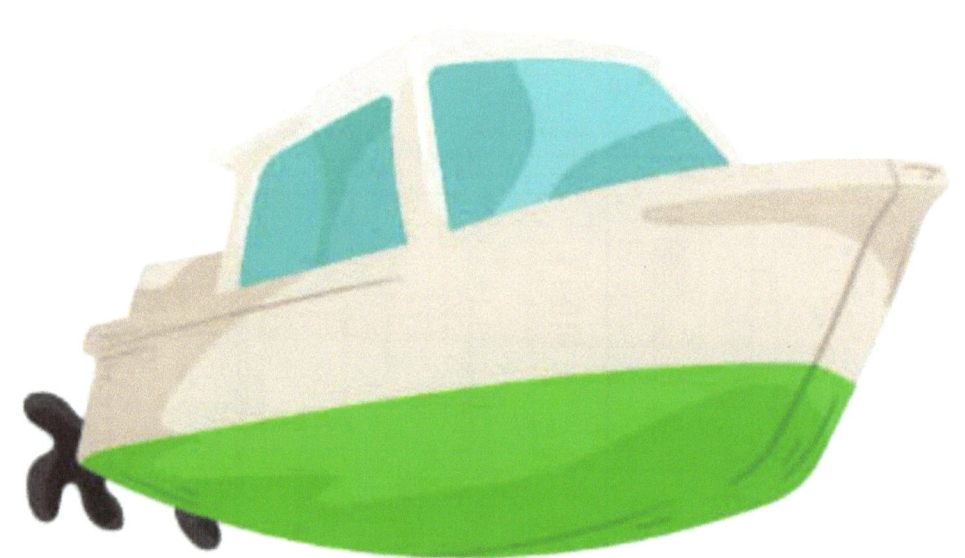

Yy

Zepellin

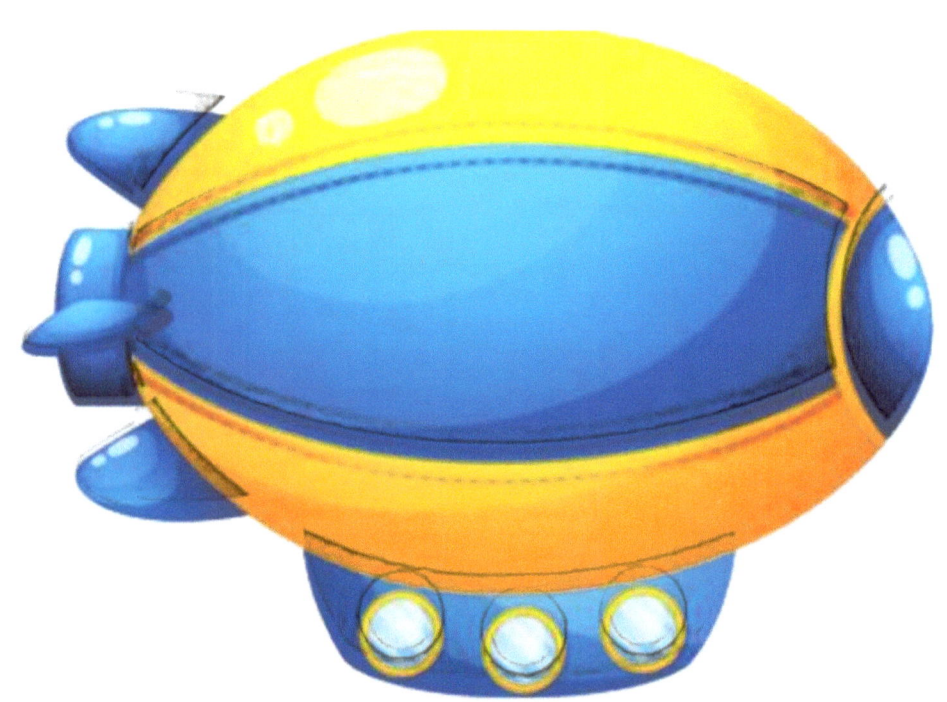

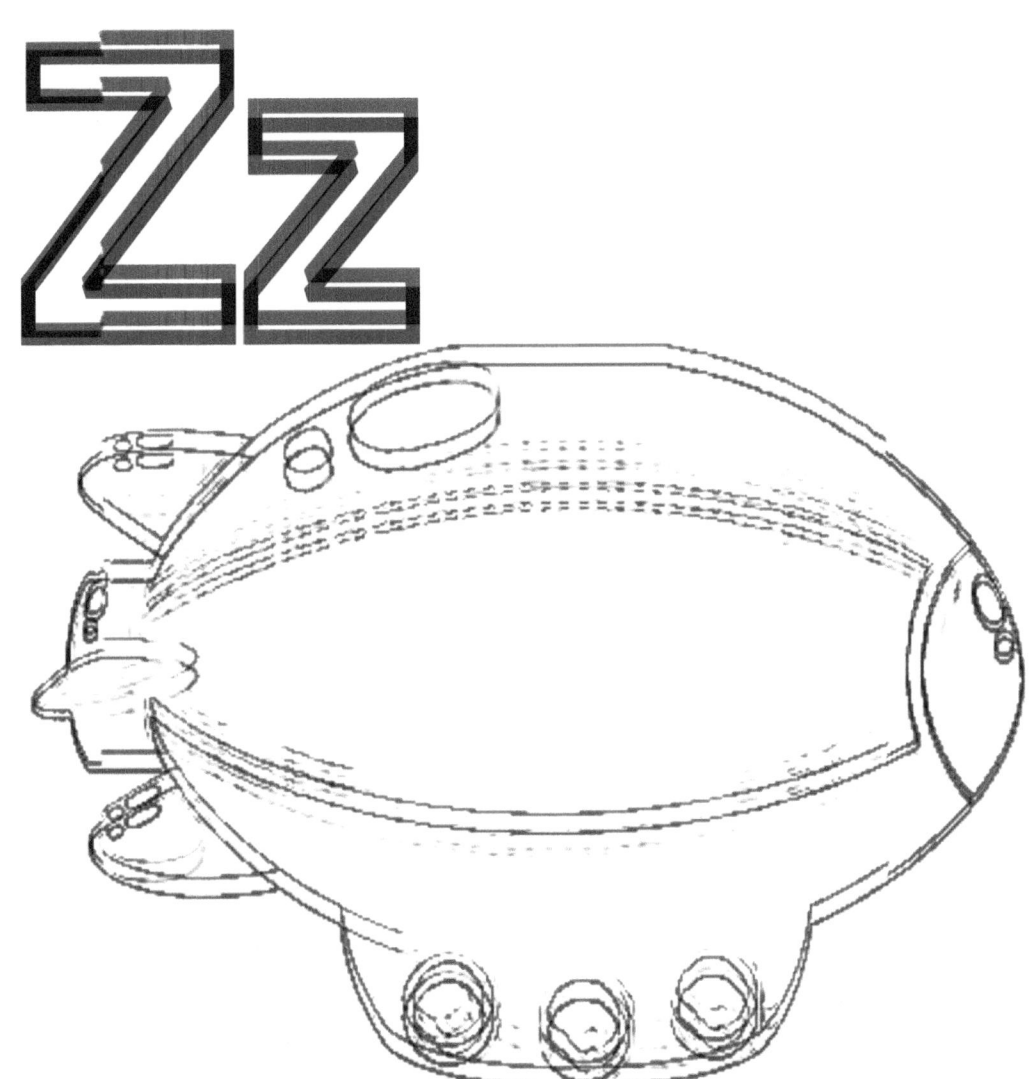

Image attribution

All colored images taken from vecteezy.com
except image 16 which is taken from freepik.com
and image 30 which is taken from pixaby.com

Other children's books by this author

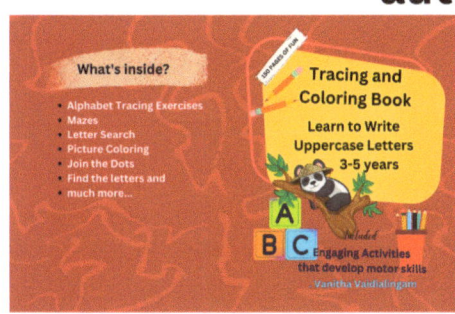
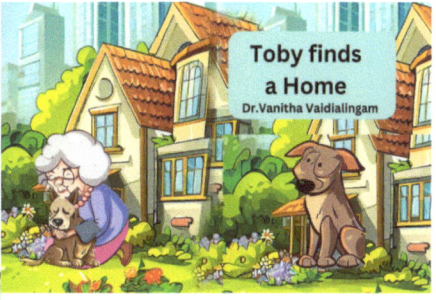
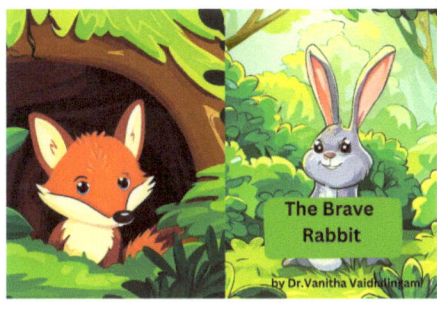

www.ingramcontent.com/pod-product-compliance
Lightning Source LLC
Chambersburg PA
CBHW051921210526
45473CB00006B/2098